# GOOD DOPE

*by*

Deshon Cooper

## *Dedication*

*Egypt and Cairo Cooper, may this book be the foundation that propels you to heights I could never reach. May this book aid you in avoiding the many mistakes I have made throughout my life.*

*Daddy loves you.*

# Table of Contents

# Introduction

First and foremost, this book is not a quick-step guide to success; there are no shortcuts. Anything that is created in this world goes through a process. The average car has about thirty thousand parts. If your car manufacturer tried to skip any of the steps required to build a vehicle, the results could be fatal. For us to turn everything that we touch into gold, there is a formula that must be followed. This formula is **DOPE**.

In this book I will teach you how to make good **DOPE**. Each one of us is divinely DOPE, which means we are **D**estined for **O**pulence, **P**rosperity and **E**xcellence. However, for us to fulfill our DOPE destiny, we must first produce good DOPE.

Good DOPE pulls us out of the darkness and into the light. The dark is a place most of us have experienced at some point throughout our lives. Some of us are still wandering around in the dark, unaware that everything we need to illuminate our world is already within us. Most of us weren't born with silver spoons. The deck has been stacked against us since the time we were born, and everything we've ever accomplished in life we had to struggle for.

In the midst of this ever-present struggle most people develop a survival mentality. People are constantly seeking ways to make surviving in their world seem easier and more comfortable. This is why people want higher-paying jobs and luxury items. We often find ourselves looking for external solutions to internal problems. We're just putting bandages on open wounds when we attempt to heal ourselves internally using external diversions such as higher-paying jobs, alcohol, drugs, and material possessions.

To find true peace and prosperity, we must produce good DOPE, which is a multilayered acronym that stands for:

**D – Direction & Discipline**

**O – Overstanding & Organization**

**P – Plans & Patience**

**E – Execution & Evaluation**

Turning everything we touch into gold also requires good DOPE. We all have it and finding it can be accomplished with two simple things: knowledge and trust.

Knowledge and trust are the foundations of good DOPE. Knowledge entails knowing who you are, knowing what your source of power is, and knowing what you want. These are the first steps in producing good DOPE. Second is trust. Trust requires us to trust our intuition and trust the process.

After we learn and trust ourselves and the source that powers our will, we must then develop OVERSTANDING. Overstanding requires us to accept the fact that we may not understand everything. There is an ayat in the Holy Quran and a verse in the Holy Bible that emphasizes us to develop overstanding.

***"But perhaps you hate a thing, and it is good for you; and perhaps you love a thing and it is bad for you. And Allah Knows, while you know not." 2:216* – Holy Quran**

***"Trust in the Lord with all your heart and lean not on your own understanding; in all your ways acknowledge him, and he will make your paths straight."* Proverbs 3:5–6**

Overstanding is one of the most important aspects of producing good DOPE because along our journey we will encounter stumbling blocks or things may happen that we will not understand. Trying to wrap our minds around everything that goes on in our life will cause more pain than progress.

Overstanding is accepting the fact that everything happens for us and not to us.

Cultivating our knowledge and trust is akin to mastering dribbling and shooting a basketball. The better a player is at dribbling and shooting, the more games they can win. The same method applies to creating gold. The more we understand ourselves and trust the power that gives us life, the more abundantly we will live. Each one of our achievements can be deduced to knowledge and trust. Knowing and trusting yourself can not only lead to a lifetime of personal success, but also set the tone for those around us to follow.

When a house is being built from the ground up, there are at least three major phases of construction: foundation, framework, and finishing. This book is comprised of three parts. Part I will focus on knowledge and trust, which is the foundation of your golden house. Part II will be the framework and part III will be all the finishing details that complete your golden temple. Although each section is intentionally short and to the point, some sections are longer than others. This does not mean that the longer sections are more important than the shorter sections, each section regardless of length is equally as important as the other sections.

*GOOD DOPE* is a formula for personal discovery. When you know who you truly are and you make good DOPE, everything you touch will turn to gold.

# PART I: Foundation

# Knowledge

*"As within so without, as above so below."*
**– The Kybalion**

For our world to lighten up, we must first turn on the light within us. There is a saying that dates to ancient Egypt: "As within so without, as above so below." As within so without means everything we are internally will be present externally. If we want peace around us, there must be peace within us.

As above, so below means everything that is above, which is mental, will also be present in the physical. The qualities we possess in the mental plane must manifest themselves in the physical plane; there is no way around it. When we closely examine our life and are completely honest with ourselves, we will realize that everything we experience stems from a good or bad thought. This is the power that all humans have; it is a gift from the source.

Before we can gain a deeper overstanding of who we are, we must connect to the source. Our source is the spirit of God. Different cultures have different names for it but in essence it is the same spirit that dwells in all of us without regard to race, religion, or nationality. Each person on this planet has access to this spirit. It is this spirit that guides us and protects us in times of danger. The voice of this spirit is intuition.

Our intuition is the force that is always there to guide us. For years I would hear people tell me that I should go within myself to find clarity. I didn't understand what that meant. I used to pray for guidance and answers to questions I had but I was expecting the guidance and the answers to be given to me from someone else, or a physical sign of some sort.

It would be years later when I finally realized that the best guidance is in fact always internal. Can you remember a time when you had a "gut feeling" that saved you from some type of danger? That feeling was your intuition. In times of danger it's easier for us to recognize this feeling/voice because it's basically yelling at us.

Intuition can not only aid us in avoiding danger, but intuition can also aid us in fulfilling our purpose. We must learn to listen.

## Using intuition to discover purpose

Everyone has something they are passionate about. Everyone has ambitions. Our dreams and passions often get swept under the rug for the sake of survival. To meet the demands of living in the society we live in, most people consume themselves with work.

Let's use Stephanie as an example.

Stephanie is a thirty-two-year-old woman who has two children that she is raising on her own. She is currently working two jobs so that she can save enough money to put a down payment on a house because she doesn't want her children to grow up in the apartment complex that she currently lives in. Stephanie loves to cook. In her spare time all she does is look up new recipes to try. All she watches is cooking shows and things involving food. Stephanie thinks this is just a hobby that she has had since she was younger but, in fact, nutrition is her purpose in life and she doesn't realize it yet.

The ego will lead us to believe that all feelings we have are our own feelings. For instance, when I discovered my purpose in life, it made sense why I always wanted to read books and learn things. It made sense why I was always the person to whom other people wanted to vent. It made sense why I was always writing something.

When you discover yourself, everything that ever happened in your life will make sense. There is a reason why Stephanie loves cooking and Steph loves playing the piano. It is not by chance that we fall in love with these things, these are intuitive feelings connected to our purpose.

When Stephanie accepts that cooking is not just a hobby of hers but it's her purpose, she will be free. She will begin to realize how many people in the world are malnourished and starving. She will realize that cooking is a God-given talent and Proverbs 18:16 says, "A man's gift makes room for him." In her case, it's "A woman's gift makes room for her," and she will realize that she doesn't have to work another job in her life so long as she uses her talents to fulfill the mission God has set for her.

## Developing intuition

It is easy to get our intuitive thoughts confused with our conscious thoughts because they both sound the same. We hear them both in our own voice. The difference lies in the feeling connected to the thought. Our intuitive voice/thought is connected to the spirit; that is why when we get an intuitive message, our heart flutters or we feel it in our stomach. Our mind has no connection, it is free, that is why we must constantly keep it in check (***Romans 12:2 "But be ye transformed by the renewing of your mind ..."***).

When we first start learning to distinguish between the two, it can become confusing, but with practice and patience you will know when your mind is playing tricks and when you are being led by the spirit.

## Affirmations for knowledge

- ✓ I am very intuitive.
- ✓ I know myself.
- ✓ I know the Creator is the source of my power.

# Trust

Trust is what everything you do is built upon. To trust fully is no easy feat. As humans we need assurance, stepping into the unknown is too frightening for some people. We need to feel like we are in control of the outcome to be secure.

There was a point along my journey when I thought I was trusting God, which I was, but I wasn't trusting fully. Trust is free from validation. The best analogy I can use for trust is the quick trip analogy.

When we fill the gas tank up in our vehicles do we check the gas hand every five minutes to see if the gas is still there? No, because we trust the gas to get us to where we must go. Most of our cars today will tell us how many miles we have until empty, and we trust that. We never second-guess it. If we fill our vehicle up with the proper gas and it says 280 miles until empty, we don't think about gas until it's time to fill up again.

When we pay a bill online, we don't go back every twenty minutes and check to make sure it's paid. We pay the bill and don't think about it until it's time to pay it again.

Why is it that when we send up our prayers, we can't trust that it will be answered the same way we trust the gas that we put in our car? If you don't worry after you fill up your tank, you shouldn't worry after you pray. Trusting is simple.

## Affirmations for trust

- ✓ I trust in my intuition.
- ✓ I trust in the Creator to guide my every step,
- ✓ I trust that all of my prayers and desires will be answered.

# PART II: DOPE FRAMEWORK

# Direction

*"Direction is more important than speed."*
**– Richard L. Evans**

Benjamin Franklin once said, "If you fail to plan, you plan to fail." Direction is the first D in DOPE because if you don't have a clear idea where you want to go, then you may turn down the wrong street. Having a goal and a plan is like having a destination and using GPS to get there. Having a goal and no plan is like having a destination and just driving around until you find it.

How would you get there if someone were to drop you off in the middle of downtown Atlanta and tell you to get to a Walmart within the next thirty minutes and you'll receive $50,000? I know some of you are thinking how easy that would be, being that you may be familiar with the area but let's assume this was your first time in Atlanta, and you didn't have the slightest clue where the nearest expressway was. What would you do? The answer is obvious, you would most likely type Walmart into your GPS, and you would most likely proceed to the nearest one. That GPS is your turn-by-turn guide to Walmart.

Let's say your goal is to be a stock trader. Stock trading is your destination (goal), and you need a GPS (plan) to get there, or you'll make a lot of wrong turns, and what should've taken you six months to learn takes you two years because you're just winging it. Our plans give us direction, tell us which way to go, and keep us grounded.

After high school, I was in limbo. I didn't know if I was coming or going, and it took me ten years to figure out what I wanted to do with my life. I consider this a reasonable amount of time compared to the number of people who never figure it out. Within those ten years, I was void of direction. Then I found myself in the tenth year.

## Understand why you want what you want

*"There is one quality which one must possess to win, and that is definiteness of purpose, the knowledge of what one wants, and a burning desire to possess it."* – **Napoleon Hill**

Sun Tzu once said, "Know yourself and know thy enemy, and in a hundred battles, you will never be in peril. When you are ignorant of the enemy but know yourself, your chances of winning or losing are equal. If ignorant both of your enemy and of yourself, you are certain in every battle to be in peril."

Knowing yourself requires knowing what you truly want from life and why. Understanding why you are doing what you're doing gives you a defense against different distractions or the temptation of giving up. For most of us, this requires some deep contemplation. You could simply write down a goal or a dream, but if it isn't truly what you want in the first place, you won't be setting yourself up for lasting success. Suppose your goals and dreams aren't aligned with your purpose. In that case, any wins will only be temporary, and you will often find yourself fighting an uphill battle or, even worse, going in circles. The goal or dream must be yours and yours alone, not something that you think you "might" need or want or something that has been forced upon you by your parents or peers. It is essential to your being, and you must do some soul-searching to find precisely what it is you want.

Ask yourself: Who am I and what is my purpose? Dig deep and uncover your *why*; by doing this, you can discover why you genuinely want these things.

Due to how the world is set up nowadays, so much of our attention is focused on survival that most of our dreams often become swept under the rug. We become locked into a routine of going to work and paying bills. Spend some time on self-reflection and recall your passions before financial and social pressures influenced your behavior. This is fundamental in understanding the life that you want to live according to your own truth and desires. As I stated earlier, it took me a while to discover my purpose, but when I knew what I truly wanted, everything became clear to me, and I knew what I had to do. When this moment of clarity comes to you, there will be no confusion about whatever steps you must take to fulfill your obligations to humanity.

**Avoid mixed signals**

In understanding why you want the things that you want it's equally important to be clear. Clarity is a sure way to avoid confusion. Indecision can lead to something undesirable or nothing at all.

A lot of people haven't gotten what they want out of life because they don't know exactly what it is that they want. One minute they want this, then they want that and then it's something else. The universe picks up all those mixed signals that the person sends out. Just imagine someone asking you for a dollar, then before you give them the dollar they change their mind and they want twelve dollars and before you give them the twelve dollars they change their mind again and ask for nine dollars. Their confusion would confuse you. Wouldn't you just wait until they make up their mind to give them anything? The same thing applies when we are asking God for something. It's best to be clear.

## Affirmations for direction

- ✓ I know who I am.
- ✓ I know where I need to be in life.
- ✓ I know how to get where I need to be.
- ✓ My path is laid out for me.
- ✓ Everything I do brings me closer to my goals.
- ✓ I am focused.
- ✓ I know who I am.

# Discipline

*"We must all suffer from one of two pains: the pain of discipline or the pain of regret. The difference is discipline weighs ounces while regret weighs tons."*
**– Jim Rohn**

The second D in DOPE is discipline. Discipline is what determines if you make it to your destination or not. There is no way around discipline. If you don't have it, accomplishing certain goals will be difficult. Developing self-discipline was the most challenging part of my journey, so it makes sense that this was the most challenging chapter for me to write. I ran from this section of the book for months and months. This book was not written in order. Initially, I made a rough outline and structural additions as time progressed. Even though this section was outlined from the beginning, this was the last section I wrote. As I'm sitting here writing, I realized that I ran from this section for two reasons. One was that this was the most challenging part of myself that I had to master. When I decided to write this book, I wanted to speak from experience and truth. How could I write about discipline if I hadn't disciplined myself?

Discipline is the master key to our desires, everything we have ever wanted and ever dreamed of lies on the other side of discipline. Discipline is a master character trait that is synonymous with truth and honesty. Those who are undisciplined are among the biggest liars in the world. Simply because they lie to themselves. If you lie to the only person who stuck by your side through the ups and downs, which is yourself, then you will lie to anybody.

I was at a point where I lied to myself constantly. I told myself I would stay out of jail, but I lied. I told myself I would get up early and work out, but when that alarm went off, I hit snooze and lied. I told myself I would eat healthier and take better care of my temple, and I lied. I told myself I would read more and lied. I told myself I would write ten pages daily and finish this book in a month, but I lied.

Lies are the fruits of an undisciplined tree. All these lies I told myself were only pulling me further away from my dreams. It's ironic how a person can be truthful with others and show up whenever they need him/her, but when it comes to themselves, they fall short. I dealt with this internal fiasco for years. I would bend over backward for anybody I cared about, but I wouldn't push over forward for myself and do a push-up.

Going from undisciplined to disciplined is a struggle, nonetheless. It takes a drill instructor twelve weeks to discipline a civilian into a warrior. After making a conscious decision to change, it took me far longer than twelve weeks to completely break some of my bad habits and replace them with something positive and constructive.

It wasn't until I read a quote by Peter Drucker, "What gets measured gets managed," did I finally begin to see a change. At the beginning of change, it's normal for us to fail more than we succeed. The only time that we really fail is when we don't correctly analyze our failures. To grow and become disciplined requires constant measurement. That's why one of the first steps we can take to become the disciplined individual we want to be is to journal every night.

## Master keys to discipline

### *Identifying your struggles*

*"By three methods we may learn wisdom, first, by reflection, which is noblest. Second, by imitation, which is easiest, and third by experience, which is bitterest."* – **Confucius**

Something magical happens when a person journals or spends some time alone reflecting on their day; it changed my life. When I started to write down what I did daily, I realized all the promises I made to myself that I was breaking. Often, we make mistakes, and we fall short of our obligations to ourselves, but the world around us is moving at such a rapid pace that we fail to acknowledge our shortcomings. Without accountability measures in place, we fall into a pattern of letting ourselves down. Having an accountability partner is an excellent tool, but at the same time, you must be accountable to yourself.

Using a journal is the easiest way to put yourself in check. Journal writing can be therapeutic. I do most of my journal writing at night as I go over my plans for the following day. When writing in my journal, I ask myself three questions.

Take ten minutes out of your night to ask yourself these three questions.

1. What did I say I was going to do today that I didn't?
2. How much time did I waste today?

2. What can I do to better myself tomorrow?

When answering these questions, it's imperative that you be as realistic with yourself as possible. You must write your answers and review them in the morning if you're serious about achieving your dreams.

*GOOD DOPE: In 30 Days* is an excellent journal to start with.

### ***Prioritizing action***

*"An ounce of action is worth a ton of theory."* – **Ralph Waldo Emerson**

After my first day of journaling and realizing how many lies I told myself on a daily basis, I made a conscious decision to make my next day lie-free. I would set out to do everything that I said I would do regardless. I realized no one was going to do it for me. Prioritizing action is the surest way to success because we never really fail at anything; we only learn what not to do next time.

For years I would jump from venture to venture, often trying new things and then getting bored and trying something else. People who didn't understand my methodology would always tell me to just stick to one thing, which is good advice. Still, I was only trying new things because I wasn't the type to sit around talking about something. I just did it; either it worked or it didn't. The best thing anyone trying to find themselves can do is just try new things; when you find the one thing that's right for you, you'll feel it. Writing and teaching were the things that I loved to do; it felt right the moment I started writing.

When prioritizing action, it's best to start small. Building momentum for change is often one of the most challenging tasks. A trick I used to help me build momentum to check off my goals was to put the simplest of tasks on my daily goal/to-do list. By writing things such as brushing your teeth, taking a shower, and washing your face on your daily task list, what you're doing is creating a habit of checking goals off. This habit will trickle over into bigger goals, and you'll get more things done before you know it.

Something as simple as making your bed as soon as you wake up can set the momentum for daily success.

### *Conquering your fears*

*"I learned that courage was not the absence of fear but the triumph over it. The brave man is not he who does not feel afraid, but he who conquers that fear."* – **Nelson Mandela**

Courageousness is one of those invaluable character traits. It isn't the absence of fear; it's the mentality that pushes you through the fear. Fear is a natural emotion, just as happiness and sadness are. There is a time to be happy, and there is a time to be sad. There is also a time to be afraid. Although fear can protect you from imminent danger, it can just as quickly cripple you.

Giving in to fear will get in the way of your goals. If you let fear of failure, fear of the future, or disappointment cripple you, you will never work on anything of value to yourself. Giving in to fear is a dream killer. If you're scared to start and give in to that fear, you will never begin.

Conquering your fears is a powerful step in your journey of self-discovery. For most of my life, I've been courageous. There have been numerous occasions where I was internally afraid. Being shot at and running from the police are some of the most frightening situations I have encountered. When you conquer that fear, it fuels you. If you've committed a crime and the police are in hot pursuit of you, freedom is on the other side of that fear. If you're in a shootout and bullets are flying past you, life is on the other side of that fear. So, I try to apply that mentality to anything I find myself being afraid of. Ask yourself, what will be the best possible outcome if I get over this fear?

### *Being content*

We all have exactly what we need; we just want more. The feeling of wanting more will never end since there is always more to be had. At some point, we must realize when we have enough and be happy with what we have.

According to Buddhism, the sensation of all desires is the end of all suffering. What that means to me is most people suffer from things that they lack or things that they feel they lack. Wanting more than you need has several consequences. Wanting more than you need can lead to wasted money, health issues, and damage to relationships. Most people misconstrue wants and needs. They often take on jobs they dread to maintain houses that are too big or to be able to drive the newest cars. They often spend more than they make to keep up with society's latest fashion and trends. I have watched videos of children in third world countries playing soccer barefoot in an open field with nothing but the bare necessities. They seem to be as happy as anything. They probably have no desire for a Rolex watch or a Mercedes Benz truck. So they are not enslaved by their constant wants. As long as their basic needs are met—shelter, water, and food—they are content.

In Thomas J. Stanley's book *The Millionaire Next Door*, he says that one of the common characteristics among America's wealthy is frugality. The wealthy understand that wanting more than you need can lead to severe problems, so they tend to live below their means. To them, what most people perceive as cheap or thrifty is a deeper understanding of necessities versus desires.

Karen is a thirty-five-year-old accountant who is in the middle of a divorce. Karen makes six figures a year. She has three cars and a five-bedroom house in an upscale neighborhood. Most of her time is spent working. Karen's husband wants a family, but Karen feels that a baby will slow down her career at the moment. Karen's desire for more money and luxury ruined her marriage.

Paul is a fifty-four-year-old retired cop. Paul is obese, and despite countless diet recommendations from his primary care physician Paul still has a hard time eating healthy. His desire for fried foods and soda has led to severe and life-threatening health issues.

The above examples illustrate how particular desires can be detrimental to one's finances as well as one's health. The problem with Karen, besides the apparent craving she has for more and more success, is she feels as though bigger and newer is indicative of better. She has this vast, luxurious house that has three of the five rooms empty. Her basement is unfinished, and she only drives one of her cars. To her, this is comforting. Karen epitomizes how wanting more than you need can lead to excessive and unnecessary expenses.

Besides absolute disdain for his health and apparent love for all things fried, the problem with Paul is that he puts his wants ahead of his needs. He takes pleasure in all the foods that are bad for him. His doctor has a recommended list of foods for him to eat and a list of foods for him to stay away from. He chose his wants over his needs, which led to severe problems.

In conclusion, there is a verse in the Holy Bible that most Christians live their lives by: Luke 12:15: "And he said unto them, 'Take care, and be on your guard against all covetousness, for one's life does not consist in the abundance of his possessions.'" This is just one of the many scriptures throughout all religions that speak of the benefits of guarding oneself against greed and desires. For many, wanting more than you need is a sin.

### *Fasting*

Fasting is also another tool that can be used to reach higher levels of discipline. If one can forgo the pleasures of food and drink for a set period, then there is no limit to anything else that can be accomplished by this person. When I committed to finishing this book, I went on an indefinite social media fast. I decided that I would not log back in to my Facebook or Instagram until this entire book was complete. This is just one example of abstinence that can help build discipline. ***For different types of fasting, see the chapter on sacrifice***.

## Affirmations for discipline

- ✓ I am who I say I am.
- ✓ I do what I say I will do.
- ✓ I am a man/woman of my word.
- ✓ My word is my bond.
- ✓ I am truthful with myself.
- ✓ I am who I say I am.

# Overstanding

*"Overstanding comes before organization. Because without overstanding, we'll find ourselves trying to organize things that only God can organize."*
**– Commissioner Coop**

The sooner we realize that some things are just beyond our understanding, the easier it will be to deal with disappointments and setbacks. I've learned that nothing ever happens to you, but everything happens for you. If you accept that statement to be true, then you have a level of overstanding. Understanding is logical. For most people, things must make sense for them to accept it.

Let's take the story of Moses and Malcolm X into account. The correlation between their stories and one having overstanding is simple. Most things are simple when we let go of our need to make sense of everything.

If Moses had not killed that man, would he have received the revelation that he received in the desert while he was running from Pharaoh?

If Malcolm X had not gone to prison, would he have taken the time to embrace the Nation of Islam and become as studious and well-spoken as he became?

When we look at each situation and try to use our understanding, then we would probably conclude that each of them made a mistake, broke the laws of the land, and eventually made the best of their situation. That's what understanding will tell us. However, overstanding will allow us to see that the Creator is in control of everything and sometimes we think we have a choice in our actions, but some things are just divine.

Where the world sees a troublemaker or a murderer, God sees one of his strongest soldiers coming closer to him. Remember nothing happens for nothing. Everything that we experience is for a reason even though sometimes we can't see the reason.

## Affirmations for overstanding

- ✓ I control what I can and let go of what I cannot.
- ✓ God is the best of planners.
- ✓ I know that everything happens for me and not to me.
- ✓ Everything that I experience is for the best.

# Organization

*"Organize your life around your dreams and watch them come true."* – **Unknown**

You can tell a lot about a person by observing their dwelling space. Is it neat? Is it cluttered? Is their closet color-coded, or are there clothes everywhere? Now this doesn't mean that one person is better than the other, but these things can be indicative of the way a person thinks. A cluttered mind will have a cluttered space. An organized mind will command organization and uniformity.

*"How you do anything is how you do everything."* – **Martha Beck**

For people who are organized mentally, there is no distinction between the things that they organize. When they wake up, they make their beds, they take care of their hygiene and then they get their day started. Before any of us can become physically organized we must first organize our minds.

Direction gives us something to organize our minds around. An organized mind with no direction can lead to obsessive-compulsive disorder (OCD).

**Personal mission statement**

In his book *The 7 Habits of Highly Effective People*, Stephen Covey expressed the importance of having a personal mission statement or a personal constitution.

Having a personal constitution has proved to be invaluable in my life. This statement gives us guidance in times of uncertainty or chaos. It underlines our governing principles and provides structure in our lives. Essentially, it is our organizational structure put into words.

It takes direction, discipline and overstanding to be organized in the right way. For some, it takes a personal constitution to enforce an organized mentality.

An example of my personal mission statement:

Spirit, mind, body. As above, so below.
Choosing what I feed my mind can affect the way I grow.
Daily, weekly, monthly. I'm always setting goals.
I'm never in a rush; I listen fast but utter slow.

## Cleanliness

Most of us have heard the saying "Cleanliness is next to godliness." Cleanliness is the highest form of organization there is. Being clean is not solely attributed to soap and water. Cleanliness is also a state of being. We clean our bodies with soap and proper diets, we clean our mind with knowledge, and we clean our souls with charity, prayer, and meditation.

## Affirmations for organization

- ✓ I am a master organizer.
- ✓ I am very clean and neat.
- ✓ My mind is organized; therefore, my life is organized.

# Planning

*"The general who wins the battle makes many calculations in his temple before the battle is fought. The general who loses makes but few calculations beforehand."*
– **Sun Tzu**

When you finally understand who you are and your purpose on this planet, clarity and calmness settle over you. At this point, it's time to develop a plan and set SMART goals. Planning is one of the most important things anyone can do in their lives. Proper planning gives you a structure for success. A day unplanned leaves room for chaos.

For years I used to get up and just wing my day. Sometimes I would wake up with a general idea of what I wanted to do, whether it was going to the studio, working out, or getting a haircut. It wasn't until I started planning my day out that I realized how much time we waste doing nothing.

While watching the Netflix series *Money Heist*, I became inspired to actually start doing some extreme planning. Even though the series is about a group of bank robbers, the leader of the group, named Professor, was one of the most calculated characters I had ever seen. He left nothing unplanned. One episode mentioned that he knew what he would wear on Friday, even though it was Monday. This was very subtle, but it motivated me to plan the way the character did in the series, and the results were phenomenal. Everything was smooth for me. I no longer had to wake up and stand in the middle of my closet, looking around and scratching my head for twenty to thirty minutes trying to decide what I wanted to wear for the day. I no longer had to worry about what I would eat for the day, I already knew. The feeling of control that planning gave me was electrifying. It kind of makes you walk and talk with more confidence.

One of the most critical aspects of planning and goal setting is ensuring your goals are SMART. SMART is an acronym that stands for:

**S** – Specific

**M** – Measurable

**A** – Attainable

**R** – Realistic

**T** – Timely

You understand that you are in charge of your own life, you carve out your own path, and that your choices have consequences. That means you must be ready to take responsibility for your actions entirely along the way. There is no more extraordinary show of integrity than when someone takes ownership of their actions, both good and bad, and shows some humility along the way. These are great qualities of true leaders, so being able to be that person who is aware of their limitations and learns from their mistakes is incredibly valuable.

Take responsibility for your life and choose to live with integrity. Don't leave any room for blaming others, that will do you no good in the long run.

An important aspect of taking responsibility for yourself and your actions is to keep your promises. If you don't keep your promises, your word will be no good, and this goes for promises to yourself and others. How will you get others to trust you if you don't trust yourself?

## Affirmations for planning

- ✓ I am a master of planning, but I know God is the best of planners.
- ✓ My plans are aligned with purpose.
- ✓ Planning is important each day.
- ✓ I am a planner.

# Patience

*"Having patience is one of the hardest things about being human. We want to do it now, and we don't want to wait.*
*Sometimes we miss out on our blessing when we rush things and do it on our own time."*
**– Deontay Wilder**

Sometimes chasing our dreams can be the most painful thing we'll ever do. Ultimately, all the pain and suffering will be worth the reward you seek. The road to our dreams is often lonely, full of setbacks, ups and downs, anxiety, regret, and depression. There were many times when I felt like giving up and many times when I questioned God. There were many times when I felt confused, lost, and completely broken. All or some of these feelings are part of the journey and are temporary. Looking back, the closer I was to fulfillment, the more hurdles I had to jump. If one can endure the pain that comes along with the journey, then the fruit on the other side is sweet and everlasting.

There is a quote that I live by:

*"The man who enjoys keenly, is subject to keen suffering; while he who feels but little pain is capable of feeling but little joy."* – **The Kybalion**

The depth of your struggles will be the height of your success! So never give up on your dreams no matter how difficult the journey may be.

## Pre-labor anxiety

There was a point in my life when I felt that I was doing everything the right way. I felt like my intentions were pure, and my actions matched that purity. Many of the negative thoughts and actions that I used to portray, I no longer projected those thoughts or actions. I was exercising regularly, meditating regularly, praying regularly, and even doing breathing exercises I read about that were meant to help with manifestation. After going through these routines and not getting the expected results, I became deeply discouraged. It made me contemplate my existence. I even began to question God, which I have sought forgiveness for. Things weren't adding up, and my confusion began to turn into frustration and rage. I wanted to quit because I was expecting immediate gratification for my efforts and wasn't receiving it. I was thinking all the meditation and manifestation talk was a bunch of BS in my head. All the books I read on the law of attraction were BS to me at that time.

Then one day, as I left the gym, I had an epiphany. An analogy about the pregnant woman came to me. This analogy I have since called pre-labor anxiety.

Imagine a woman being five months pregnant and desperately wanting to have her baby; she can't wait to see her first son. So, she begins meditating, fasting, and doing all types of yoga exercises in preparation for delivery. After a few weeks of going through her routines, she starts getting anxious because the baby hasn't come yet. After another week or so of following her routine, she becomes frustrated and starts questioning everything she thought she knew. Because all she wants is her son, and her intentions and thoughts have been pure up until then. Not once did it dawn on her that no matter how much meditation she does, everything has a process that we must trust and follow.

Sitting in the car and thinking about the pregnant woman and how much I was acting like her gave me a paradigm shift. Like her, I was seven months pregnant and became frustrated because I wasn't giving birth to my dreams prematurely.

We have to trust the process. Just as a woman must endure pain and discomfort for a set number of weeks to give birth to a baby, we, too, must endure for a set number of weeks to give birth to a dream.

## Pre-harvest anxiety

Imagine someone having a dream of growing their own food and so one day, they finally decide to follow their dreams. They start planting potato seeds first and water them every day for a week. On the eighth day, they come out to check their crop and see nothing but dirt, so they become discouraged, frustrated, and confused. The worse thing this new gardener can do is allow his/her frustration and confusion to cause them to stop properly tending to their crop, regardless of what they see. I'm no expert gardener, but I know you must water a crop for more than a week to see anything desirable. Secondly, potatoes grow under the dirt, so no matter how many days you water them, the treasure will always be hidden in the soil.

This analogy can easily be applied to our life on two levels.

1. After we plant the seed of our dream, we must continue to water for however long it takes to produce the crop of our imagination.
2. Some crops aren't visible on the surface. Every seed we plant in the ground doesn't grow tall and colorful. So, every seed we sow in our life doesn't develop into Maseratis and mansions. Some seeds grow internally and become knowledge, wisdom, and understanding.

## Meditation

*"If you want to conquer the anxiety of life, live in the moment, live in the breath."* – **Amit Ray**

There are many ways to develop patience. One of the most profound and life-changing ways to do this is through meditation. This involves breathing techniques, guided imagery, and other practices designed to reduce stress on the body and mind. Meditation calms the mind and relieves stress by focusing on breathing.

If you can sit and focus on your breath for ten minutes a day, this can help to reduce mild anxiety and depression.

## A brick a day

Rome wasn't built in one day. As often as I've heard someone tell me that, it didn't stop the anxiety I would feel whenever I thought about how much work I had to put in to get where I needed to be.

Feeling overwhelmed with potential tasks is quite common among all people. The best defense for becoming too anxious and allowing the thought of what could be to stress you is to lay a brick a day.

Laying a brick a day means taking things one day at a time, doing whatever you can do for that day, and not allowing whatever is left undone to deter you. If one were to lay a brick a day at a consistent pace, when one looks up, one would have built an entire mansion.

When ascending a flight of stairs, you don't tend to stress out and worry about how you will get to the top. You just climb one step at a time. Be easy on yourself, take it one step at a time, and lay one brick per day, and you will be that much closer to all that you desire.

## Affirmations for patience

- ✓ I am patient.
- ✓ Everything happens precisely when it's supposed to.
- ✓ Nothing that's meant for me can ever miss me.
- ✓ I believe in divine timing.
- ✓ I am patient.

# Execution

*"Take time to deliberate, but when the time for action has arrived, stop thinking and go in."* – **Napoleon Bonaparte**

What separates those who wish to do something from those who do it? Execution. If you never take a shot, you'll never hit a target. If you want to reach a goal, identifying it is the first step, then you must take the other necessary steps to make it happen. Don't sit around waiting for something to fall on your lap. One of the most challenging life lessons for me to accept was there is never truly a perfect time to do what you need to do; the time is now. The Roman emperor Marcus Aurelius said that most men can be great today, but instead, they choose tomorrow. Tomorrow is the busiest day of the year, and tomorrow may never come for some.

Nevertheless, there are times when taking action can be foolish, and waiting can be wise. A concrete plan can help us determine when action or inaction is necessary.

# Evaluation

*"Evaluation is creation: hear it, you creators! Evaluating is itself the most valuable treasure of all that we value. It is only through evaluation that value exists: and without evaluation the nut of existence would be hollow. Hear it, you creators!"*

**– Friedrich Nietzsche**

Evaluation is the last aspect of producing good DOPE because what gets measured gets managed properly. If there are ever any problems in your life and you feel overwhelmed, depressed, or anxious, the best thing to do is evaluate your DOPE. Good DOPE is never anxious, depressed or overwhelmed.

One of the best forms of evaluation is setting goals and going over them daily. I call this *preventative evaluation*.

Preventative evaluation is when you check yourself daily to ensure that you are staying on course. Straying away from your goals and plans will lead to anxiety, depression, and regret. After you begin feeling these counterproductive feelings, then you must do an *overall evaluation* to see where you went wrong.

An overall evaluation, or OE, is a series of questions that allows you to check every aspect of your DOPE. Checking every aspect of your DOPE shows you exactly where a problem may be.

Below is a series of questions that will pinpoint any problems in your DOPE. Answer these questions as truthfully as possible for best results.

*Do I know where I want to go?*
*Do I know how I will get there?*
*Am I trying to control things I have no control over?*
*Am I being impatient?*
*Are my thoughts, dreams and goals organized?*
*Is my life organized?*
*Have I been acting on my plans?*
*Have I been checking myself daily?*

For example, let's say you feel overwhelmed and you have no idea what's going on in your life. You would sit down with a piece of paper and write down the questions above. Usually, we get overwhelmed because we are unprepared. Things start coming at us left and right that we didn't plan for, and it throws us off track, which then leads to being overwhelmed.

By answering these questions, you will see that you may be overwhelmed because you are trying to control things you have no control over, or you may know where you want to go in life, but you are confused about how to get there. Whatever the case may be, use these questions to pinpoint any problems and make the necessary adjustments.

# Part III: Finishing Details

# Forgiveness

*"It's not an easy journey, to get to a place where you forgive people. But it is such a powerful place because it frees you."*
**– Tyler Perry**

Holding grudges and harboring hate is a sure way to prolong your journey. It costs much more energy to hate than to love. There was a point in my life when I was completely unforgiving. As a child I was sexually victimized, and I carried this trauma with me well into my twenties and almost my thirties. Being a victim of sexual abuse is one of the most traumatizing things any child can go through because it doesn't really begin affecting you until you are older. People are affected in a number of ways; some people become very promiscuous, some people become very aggressive, some people become homosexual and some people even take their own lives. The best route to healing childhood trauma is acceptance and forgiveness. For years I compartmentalized the abuse that I experienced until it almost wasn't real but doing this caused more damage than it helped because my temper was short, I didn't like to be touched, and I was incapable of being a good man in relationships. I couldn't see myself settling down, I didn't complete tasks, and the list goes on. It wasn't until I went and reread the four agreements that I allowed myself to forgive. After I forgave everybody, including myself, for everything I had been holding on to, I felt a weight lifted from my heart. I was happier, and being happier raised my vibration, aiding me in working toward my dreams.

Being locked inside a cell and not hearing from people who you might've helped in some way when you were free can cause a lot of pent-up aggression. It becomes easy to develop a me-against-the-world attitude when going through certain situations alone. The best thing we can do is to forgive and move on; it's lighter on the soul when we let things go. Sometimes we aren't in a position to receive blessings because of all the emotional baggage we hold on to from past situations. Let go!

## Master key to forgiveness

One hundred and thirty-four years ago, German philosopher Friedrich Nietzsche said, "*Was mich nicht umbringt, macht mich starker,*" which translates to "*What doesn't kill me, makes me stronger.*"

The master key to forgiveness is understanding that everything we go through works for us, not against us. Sometimes people have wronged us, and we can only think about what they did to us, not how much stronger and wiser it made us.

When we embrace this way of thinking, forgiveness becomes effortless. We can now appreciate all the tough lessons we learned from being let down by others and ourselves.

Most people ideally would want the perfect relationship; however, sometimes, we must go through a few bad relationships to recognize the person who complements us the most. With this mentality, we can easily forgive those who have cheated on us and lied to us.

Ruminating over past events or decisions won't help you move forward in achieving your goals. You must be able to embrace your past choices, mistakes, and even situations that affected you that were out of your control. Doing this allows you to take control of your own future. To do this wholeheartedly, you must let go. I chose to forgive myself for my past mistakes, and this helped me have the strength to move forward. You cannot move forward if you are obsessing over the past, so live in your present and choose to let go of your regrets. You can do this through journaling, meditation, or even seeking professional help if you need it. Still, one thing is sure, if you continue to dwell on the past negatively, you won't be able to create a positive future for yourself.

## Affirmations for forgiveness

- ✓ I forgive myself for my past.
- ✓ I release resentment and pain from my body.
- ✓ I accept my past and learn from it.
- ✓ I have to courage to move forward.
- ✓ I am worthy of kindness and compassion.
- ✓ I am capable of moving beyond my own mistakes.
- ✓ The past is done; I choose to live in the present.

# Sacrifice

*"I think that the good and the great are only separated by the willingness to sacrifice."*
**– Kareem Abdul-Jabbar**

Sacrifice and discipline go hand in hand; you can't have one without the other. Both sacrifice and discipline build off each other. What are you willing to give up in the pursuit of your dreams?

In the way in which the universe works, nothing comes without sacrifice. To get something, you have to give something. When a woman conceives a child, she sacrifices her body for nine months to deliver her baby. When someone is on a diet to lose weight and get in better shape, they are sacrificing the pleasure of eating foods that may be good to them but not good for them.

Fasting is the ultimate sacrifice. Fasting has been a secret gateway to manifestation and enlightenment in many different religions worldwide, from Buddhism and Judaism to Islam and Christianity.

"Moses was there with the Lord forty days and forty nights without eating bread or drinking water. And he wrote on the tablets the words of the covenant – the Ten Commandments" (Exodus 34:28).

*"O you who believe, fasting is prescribed for you as it was prescribed for those before you, that you may develop God-consciousness."* – **Holy Quran 2:183**

Fasting is not just limited to abstaining from food and water. I personally took a social media fast while I finished this book and worked on manifesting my dreams. Some days I would fast from food and only drink water. I also fasted from excessive sexual pleasures in the pursuit of my dreams. There are many variations to fasting, and there are many different things we should sacrifice if we are serious about manifesting our dreams. With faith and sacrifice, nothing is impossible.

Limiting or absolving yourself of the vices that tempt you, like certain foods or habits, will help you build self-discipline. Know your temptations and weaknesses. Is it checking social media every few seconds or overspending when you go to the store? If you find yourself indulging in behaviors that will get in the way of achieving your goals, recognize them and consciously remove or limit them from your life. This is why daily or weekly self-assessments are essential. Replacing bad habits is more manageable than quitting them cold turkey.

## Affirmations for sacrifice

- ✓ I release the things that do not serve me.
- ✓ I am firm in my desire for change.
- ✓ I will do what I have to do to get where I want to be.

# Gratitude

*"Gratitude is the healthiest of all human emotions. The more you express gratitude for what you have, the more likely you will have even more to express gratitude for."*

**– Zig Ziglar**

"Counting your blessings" is an age-old saying for a reason. Practicing gratitude, whether journaling about it daily or simply stating it aloud, can significantly affect your outlook on life. Journaling puts situations into perspective. Being grateful for family, having groceries, or even something as simple as enjoying the benefits that rain brings to the earth is something to journal about. Anything that brings you a small amount of joy or happiness is something to be grateful for. Focusing on the positive and connecting with what you are thankful for will change your attitude into a more positive one and attract more of it in your own life.

Acknowledging what you're grateful for fosters optimism, and this attitude will help you reach your goals and dreams.

## Two ways to express gratitude

Here are two ways that you can express gratitude daily for you to reach your fullest potential:

1. See the good in everything.
2. Be generous.

Seeing the good in everything

It can be challenging not to be hard on yourself. You are your harshest critic, after all. When we recognize beauty in all things, beautiful things start to happen. People will only treat you how you treat yourself. If you look in the mirror and focus on the things you don't like about yourself, you are not setting yourself up for long-term success.

When we find fault in others, others find fault in us. It's the karmic law. We reap what we sow. When we sow seeds of gratitude and happiness, they return to us in abundance.

Seeing the good in other people is also a meaningful expression of gratitude. People do things I don't like all the time. I had to learn not to dwell on the negative aspects and try to see their beauty, if possible. Nobody is perfect. Most people in our lives have something that we can be grateful for, regardless of how annoying they can be from time to time.

This doesn't mean that we are naïve and allow people to get over on us by being blind to their negativity. It just means that we understand we will be scrutinized in the same manner we scrutinize others.

## Be generous

*"The wise man does not lay up his own treasures.*
*The more he gives to others,*
*the more he has for his own."* – **Lao Tzu**

We've all heard the saying you have to give to receive; it's no wonder why people who do good deeds for others are among the most blessed individuals on this planet. Giving charity is held in high regard in many religions throughout the world. Giving charity regularly is cleansing to the soul. It reverses some of the bad karma we may have built up and replaces it with peace and abundance. However, you must give with pure intentions and believe that one day you be repaid for your contributions. Don't expect to give a homeless man one dollar today and win a lottery jackpot tomorrow, even though this is possible. Don't expect it to happen that way because if it doesn't happen the way you expect it to, you'll become discouraged.

## Affirmations for gratitude

- ✓ I am grateful for the love from my family.
- ✓ I am grateful that I have shelter and food.
- ✓ I am grateful that I am free.
- ✓ I am grateful for everything good that awaits me today.
- ✓ I am thankful for myself and everything that I am capable of.
- ✓ I am grateful for this beautiful universe.

# Letting Go of Your Dreams

To achieve your dreams, you have to let them go. As long as you're holding on to them in your head, you're not allowing those thoughts to manifest. A thought cannot be in two places at once.

Just imagine if Leonardo da Vinci only thought about painting the *Mona Lisa* or Tupac only thought about recording "Brenda's Got a Baby." These thoughts must be let go of and acted upon to transition from the mental realm to the physical realm.

Think back to a time in your life when you may have been singing a song in your head or thinking about something, and someone around you began singing the song aloud or speaking about the very thing you were just thinking about, and you said, "I was just thinking about that." Since thoughts are energy, what actually happens is your thoughts are transferred, and someone around you picks up your mental signal.

Another example is when you are looking for something and can't seem to find it, no matter how hard you think about where it could be. The minute you stop thinking about finding whatever you are looking for, boom, there it is.

I've come to realize that the fastest way to get some of the things we think about is not to think about them, let the thought travel to its appropriate place, and you'll have all that your heart desires.

There are many examples of this in everyday life.

If you're still not convinced, here is a small experiment.

**Step 1:** Spend twenty minutes watching the clock, watch, or even the time on your phone. Take note of how long those twenty minutes seemed.

**Step 2:** Set a timer for twenty minutes and then find something to do until the timer goes off. You can do anything. Take a shower, read a book, cook food, and watch a movie. When the timer goes off, note how long the twenty minutes seem.

You will notice that the twenty minutes you watched the clock seemed as if it took a lifetime to pass, and the twenty minutes you were occupied went by extremely fast. Could this be because you were thinking about one and not the other?

## The power of vibration

Everything in the universe is made up of energy; what differentiates everything from something else is its vibration. These vibrations are caused by atoms that all vibrate at different speeds and frequencies. Everything has a vibration; trees, people, animals, even thoughts and emotions.

To harness the powers of manifesting, we must raise our vibration. Higher vibrations are associated with love, compassion, and kindness. In contrast, lower vibrational frequencies are related to negative emotions like fear, anger, shame, or guilt. The higher we vibrate, the more positivity and abundance we attract into our lives. The more we positively affect the people around us, the easier it is for us to bring our dreams to fruition.

Our minds cannot always understand or comprehend the divine aspects of the universe and God. Your logical brain will always insist on doing things its own way and taking the easiest route.

# Dissociation

*"Show me a man's friends, and I'll show you his future."*
**– Unknown**

I chose this section to be last because if you forget any of the other lessons in this book, I don't want you to forget this. One of the most important things we can do to pursue our dreams is to align with like-minded individuals. The people around us can either harm us or help us.

Often, it's family and friends we cherish the most who mean us no good, and this doesn't mean that they seek to intentionally harm us. It just means that our path is much different from theirs, and they are often stuck in their destructive ways. As much as we would love to see them change, the best thing you can do is disassociate yourself from anything that doesn't align with your mission.

Disassociating yourself from family members and people you've been friends with for years is no easy feat. The first step to disassociation is to identify your reason. It's easier when you have a definitive reason. Maybe you're on a health journey, and your friends love getting together to eat pizza and drink soda. You're saving money to start a business, and your friends go to the club every weekend. These are common reasons for dissociation, while others can be more personal.

Dissociation doesn't have to be an ugly thing. How do you dissociate from someone? There are three ways to do this, and you can do whichever is more comfortable for you. First, you can begin by letting them know how you feel. You don't owe them an explanation. Be calm and move on. If you don't want to openly end your relationship with this person, slowly remove yourself from their life. Start by declining any of their invitations, respond to their phone calls or messages less frequently, and, as time goes on, even less. Remember, you don't owe them an explanation, so you do what you need to do for your own mental health and self-preservation. And lastly, you can just completely cut them out if you can. Cut all contact and let it go. Set your boundaries and stick to them.

It can be as easy as you simply declining to go out. You don't always have to say, "I'm staying away from you guys because we are not on the same path right now," which could cause resentment. Do whatever makes you comfortable, but whatever you do, don't associate yourself with people who are not on the same sheet of music as you.

If people around you aren't on your level and take more energy from you than they give, you need to walk away from them. If you have people in your life who are self-absorbed, manipulative, emotionally abusive, or not trustworthy, get them out of your life. That kind of negativity is a recipe for disaster. Some people love to create drama and thrive on conflict. Again, get these people out of your life and move on.

## Release that which is holding you back

This isn't just about letting go of the toxic people in your life who no longer serve you. You also have to let go of thoughts and habits that no longer serve you. Let go of the negativity. During this process, recognize that, like all things, there will be challenges that you will have to face on this journey. There will be things that are good to us but not necessarily good for us. Sometimes we must venture outside our comfort zones to see our desired success.

## Surround yourself with positivity: refocus your energy

A big part of dissociating is refocusing your energy and putting your efforts into creating and maintaining positive relationships and thoughts. Surround yourself with people who are grinding the same way you are and trying to be better themselves. Their attitude to life and what they're trying to achieve for themselves will inspire you. Most importantly, you'll enjoy being around them. Being around others who are positive is infectious. What you choose to focus on, including your relationships, is a reflection of you. So raise your standards, leave those who dwell in fear, worry, or ignorance, and spend your time with people who are going after their dreams.

## Be mindful of who you have sex with

Sexual energy is one of this planet's most powerful and sacred energies. The person we choose to lie down and exchange that energy with is the most important in our life. Most times, people get caught up in the pleasure side of sex and are ignorant of the other side.

There is a physical and spiritual exchange when you have sex with someone, especially unprotected. You are tying your soul with theirs. Their good and bad energy is now yours and vice versa. Choosing the right partner can be the stepping stone to reaching your highest potential or a stepping stone to failure. Sexual partners either give you life or drain it from you. Choose wisely.

## Affirmations for associations

- ✓ I release things and people that no longer serve me.
- ✓ I am beneficial to everyone around me.
- ✓ And everyone around me is beneficial to me.
- ✓ I release people and things that no longer serve me.

# Mentality

*"Not everyone gets to be a winner unless they choose to be. Winning is a mentality."* – **Valentin Chmerkovskiy**

The proper mentality is vital for good DOPE. Once you shift your focus inward, you will realize that all your problems are inside you. Anything you do outside of yourself to fix your problems will only be a patch job leading to more problems. That is like painting a car with motor issues thinking the paint job will help it drive better instead of popping the hood and fixing what needs to be fixed. So, until their mentality is adjusted, it doesn't matter how much money a person comes across; they still will not be able to reach their fullest potential.

An example of this is people who are not mentally organized having trouble staying physically organized no matter how hard they try. People's houses, cars, and closets are cluttered because their mind is cluttered. That is why the clutter usually piles back up within days after they attempt to declutter their spaces. Because only decluttering the mind leads to an organized home, a clean car, and a neat closet. Therefore mentality, the first of the three fundamental principles, is the most important.

Being poor is not a condition but a mentality. Mentality can be defined as how a person thinks. People can be born into poverty, but only poor thinking will keep them there. People confuse struggling with being broke. Struggling is a part of the process; being broke is the problem.

A person struggling in a poverty-stricken environment can rise above their environment if they don't have a poor or broke mentality. This principle has been taught for centuries by those who understood the power of the mind. The Holy Bible says, "As a man thinketh, so is he." Fully understanding this tactic is the first step toward true success and longevity.

From an early age, I was groomed to be a hustler. In retrospect, if I did not adjust my mentality, I might have ended up in the same position as some of my peers who feel victim to unfortunate circumstances. My father served a prison sentence for armed robbery from when I was born until I was ten.

As young boys, our first role models are usually our fathers or celebrities. Growing up, all my role models were gangsters or drug dealers.

There are a lot of things that I wish someone had taught me early on. Most of the lessons I learned in life I had to learn them hard. It wasn't until my mid-twenties that I began to unlearn some of the self-defeating habits I picked up along the way, and I started to see a change in my life. However, the results I sought weren't instantaneous. I was headed in a new direction because many of my surroundings and desires were slowly beginning to change.

Three critical mental adjustments need to be made to achieve lasting success.

## Three key mentality adjustments

Three essential mental adjustments must be made to achieve lasting success in the physical world.

1. Adjust the way we think about being rich versus poor.
2. Adjust the way we think about money and saving.
3. Adjust the way we think about time.

### *Rich vs poor*

We now understand that poor is a mentality, and by adjusting our mentality, we can overcome any obstacle. People are also confused about being rich. Rich people only have money. Rich is a lifestyle. Rich people make a lot of money and spend a lot of money. They leave nothing to their children's children. Being wealthy should be the goal. Wealth is sustainable; wealth is transferrable. To create generational wealth, one must think like the wealthy think. Wealthy people are excellent managers of money. They know how to make money and make it grow.

Rich people are excellent money earners. They know how to get out here and make more money; however, once their finances increase, so does their spending. That is an example of rich people with poor thinking. Instead of getting more money and buying a newer car or a bigger house, why not invest the extra so that the extra money makes you extra money? The more money you make before upgrading your lifestyle, the better you will be able to sustain your upgrade for years to come. What is the point in saving your money for a down payment on a bigger house and a fancier car only for something unforeseen to happen? Maybe you lose your job, or perhaps the economy crashes, and now you must foreclose on your home, and your car is up for repo?

We also must realize the world we live in now differs from when we were children. Symbols of success are different as well. A new foreign car no longer means a person is wealthy. People will spend $500 on a pair of shoes and only have $5,000 to their name. That's a poor mentality. Give a person with a poor mentality $1 million. After they spend their first dollar, they will never be a millionaire again until they change their mentality. From the first minute that million hits their account, they will start subtracting, not even thinking about multiplying.

The average car of millionaires in America is a Ford. Most millionaires do not spend their money in designer stores. So why do a lot of people who don't even have a quarter of a million dollars saved feel the need to wear designer labels only?

Wanting to do better is the first step. Understanding that many of the things we were taught about rich and poor must be unlearned and relearned for us to develop properly. Growing up, it was drilled into most kids that they needed to finish school and go to college to get a good job and succeed. We were not taught about the importance of credit or how getting a trade could make you more money than getting a degree. Neither were we taught that making a lot of money and spending a lot of money is almost the same as not having any money at all. The only difference is the person may be more comfortable. However, in reality, they are still poor due to their mentality.

In 2018 I had just come home from prison, and within a month of me coming home, I had a construction job paying $22 an hour with guaranteed overtime every week. I stayed employed there for about six months before I quit. There are two gems hidden in that story.

1. Fresh out of prison, I could get a job making more money than most people with degrees. This made me think if people go to college to make more money, why don't they just get a trade and work these blue-collar jobs that are paying the big money if money is the motive?
2. Earning $22 an hour, guaranteed overtime, and health insurance is an excellent job for a twenty-six-year-old. Most people would feel as if they made it and would be content to work their way up the company ladder and get a house, start a family, and

retire. Nothing is wrong with it if that's the person's dream. However, I was far too ambitious to continue trading my time for money inside a company. Why settle for $22 an hour when you can make $22 million a year if you apply yourself just as hard as you apply yourself for other people (the reason I quit).

### *Money and saving*

To reach the levels we desire in life, we have to change our mentality about money and saving. How we think about money and how we think about saving will determine how much success we will see. Money is not meant to be worked for; money is intended to work for you. Our spending habits will change when we think of money as a tool instead of a reward. A reward is defined as something given in recognition of one's service, so is your company not rewarding you for doing your job?

Suppose a person works forty hours a week, and when they get their paycheck (reward), they decide they want to do something nice and buy some shoes or go out for dinner and a movie. They may even be saving their money for a trip, but either way, what they are really doing is creating a dependency system. By taking the money a company pays you and wasting it, you are putting yourself in a position of "having to work" to continue supporting your wasteful habits. Most people I know with nine-to-fives hate their job, but they are stuck, and they will continue to be stuck until they change their *mentality* about *saving*. Let us put this into a new perspective.

Paul and Jacob both work for a telecommunications company. They each make $17 an hour and work forty hours a week. After taxes, each one of them brings home roughly $500 a week. With monthly expenses totaling about $1,500, excluding groceries, they both have about $500 a month to play with. Paul has been reading books in his spare time and fully understands the three fundamentals of success. He has been studying ways to create a couple of multiple streams of income so he can leave his job and live his life to its fullest potential. Paul has a budget sheet, a goal, and a detailed plan to reach his goal. All his extra money goes into his savings. He is not eating out and buying shoes and clothes. Paul is wholly focused on his plans; he has tunnel vision.

Jacob, on the other hand, has vices. He likes to smoke when he gets off, and he stops to buy fast food most days on his way home. On the weekend, Jacob goes out to a local bar and has a few drinks, and he prides himself on being fresh. Jacob saves a little and spends a lot. He dips in his savings account quite often for things that are not important, even though he always puts the money back. Jacob has no real plan. He wants to invest in stocks as well as start a business. Still, he is easily distracted, so he spends more time scrolling through social media than figuring out what type of business he wants to start. Jacob lives paycheck to paycheck; everything he has coming in is going out. He is doomed to fail if he does not change his thoughts about money and saving.

People who save money just to save it must also adjust their mentality about money and saving. Having $50,000 in your savings account and zero dollars invested is no good. That $50,000 will not hold the same value for ten years from the day you started saving it. Inflation will dwindle your savings without you even realizing it. Just imagine how having $100 fifteen years ago could buy you quite a few things; that same $100 now does not come close to the value it had back then. This is inflation.

All of this can be eliminated by saving with a purpose. When you save with a purpose, you have a clear, definitive goal that you are trying to reach, making it easier to curb distractions as they arise. Saving with a purpose means you are saving, and you have a reason why you are saving; such as saving for a down payment on a rental property or saving to open up a barbershop.

### *Time*

Even though time is an illusion, it is human's most valuable commodity. Time cannot be replaced, nor do we know when it will end; for some, it's long, and for others, it's shortened. The only thing on this earth guaranteed to us all, wealthy or penniless, young or old, brown or white, is death. Yet we live our lives as if we will physically be here forever. We can never get the time we wasted back. The sooner we adjust our mentality about time, the better we will feel about it as we grow older. You don't want to be sixty years old thinking about everything you should've done differently or all the time you wasted doing nothing. Value your time now. One of the best things we can do with our time is to put ourselves in a position to live out our true purpose. There is no way anyone can convince me that we were born to go to work, pay bills and then die so our children can continue the cycle. Therefore, if we are trading our time for money, we are not able to live out our purpose or chase our dreams. That coincides with understanding money and how to use it correctly. Money is a tool. When you get money and put that money to work, you create a machine that will take care of you while you walk in your purpose. The less you trade your time for money, the more time you have to create a legacy that will outlive you. *Spend your time wisely*. Those of us who are successful are masters of time management.

Even if you temporarily have to trade your time for money to support your dream, you must manage the time you are not working. Most people who trade their time for money get off work and they are tired, so they cannot wait to rest and relax because they know they must be back at work the next day.

Those individuals who value their time are the ones who get off work and start working on themselves just as hard. They go home, study, plan, and do whatever is necessary to relieve themselves of the burden of having to work for someone else. They don't have any time to waste; they are goal-oriented and on a mission.

## Affirmations for mindset, money, and time

- ✓ I am confident in my ability to make the right decisions for my well-being.
- ✓ My mind is my greatest weapon.
- ✓ I think only the best thoughts.
- ✓ I am excited about positive change.
- ✓ I release the things that no longer serve me.
- ✓ I am a master of time and money.
- ✓ I substitute poor thinking for wealthy thinking.

# Recommended reading list

1. *GOOD DOPE: In 30 Days* by Deshon Cooper
2. *Your Life: Why It Is the Way It Is and What You Can Do About It – Understanding the Universal Laws* by Bruce McArthur
3. *The Game of Life and How to Play It* by Florence Scovel Shinn
4. *The Way of the Superior Man* by David Deida
5. *The 7 Habits of Highly Effective People* by Stephen Covey
6. *Mastery* by Robert Greene
7. *The Alchemist* by Paulo Coelho
8. *The Art & Science of Respect: A Memoir* by James Prince
9. *Rich Dad, Poor Dad* by Robert T. Kiyosaki
10. *The Richest Man in Babylon* by George S. Clason
11. *The Secret* by Rhonda Byrne
12. *The Spook Who Sat by the Door* by Sam Greenlee
13. *Think and Grow Rich* by Napoleon Hill

14. *The 22 Immutable Laws of Marketing: Violate Them at Your Own Risk* by Al Ries
15. *Black Privilege: Opportunity Comes to Those Who Create It* by Charlamagne Tha God
16. *Unlimited Power* by Tony Robins
17. *The 50th Law* by Robert Greene
18. *The Master Key System* by Charles F. Haanel
19. *African Holistic Health* by Llaila Afrika
20. *From Niggas to Gods* by Akil
21. *Who Moved My Cheese* by Spencer Johnson
22. *How to Win Friends and Influence People* by Dale Carnegie
23. *The E-Myth Revisited* by Michael Gerber
24. *The Body That Keeps Score* by Bessel van der Kolk MD

Printed by Libri Plureos GmbH in Hamburg,
Germany